NIGERIA

One Nation, Many Cultures

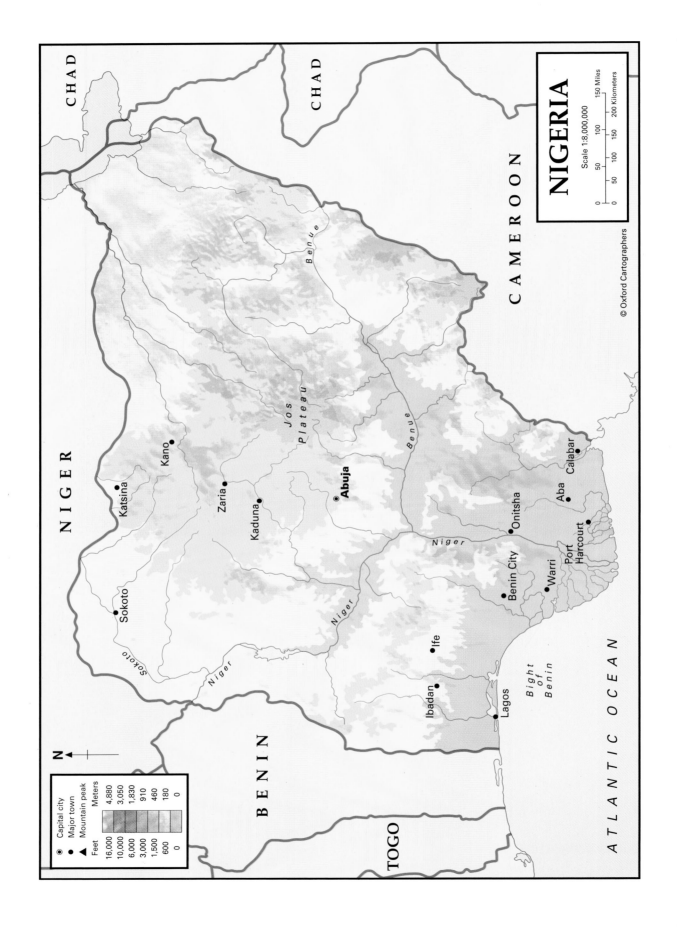

CHAD

CHAD

NIGER

BENIN

TOGO

CAMEROON

© Oxford Cartographers

ATLANTIC OCEAN

Katsina

Kano

Sokoto

Zaria

Kaduna

Abuja

Ife

Ibadan

Lagos

Benin City

Warri

Onitsha

Aba

Port Harcourt

Calabar

Bight of Benin

Jos Plateau

Benue

Benue

Niger

Niger

Niger

Sokoto

N

NIGERIA

Scale 1:8,000,000

150 Miles

50 100

200 Kilometers

50 100 150

0

0

Capital city		
Major town		
Mountain peak		
Feet	Meters	
16,000	4,880	
10,000	3,050	
6,000	1,830	
3,000	910	
1,500	460	
600	180	
0	0	

EXPLORING CULTURES OF THE WORLD

NIGERIA
One Nation, Many Cultures

Hassan Adeeb and Bonnetta Adeeb

BENCHMARK BOOKS

MARSHALL CAVENDISH
NEW YORK

*For their generous assistance and expert advice, the authors wish to thank
Augustine Konneh, Assistant Professor of African, Caribbean,
and World Histories, Morehouse College, Atlanta, Georgia;
and Clarence G. Seckel, Jr., Curriculum Coordinator in the Social Studies,
East Saint Louis School District 189, East Saint Louis, Illinois.*

TO OUR DAUGHTERS NAFISA, SHANTA, AND MEROE

We would like to thank the following people for their help: Ma Lee Jordan for watching the girls while we spent hours at the computer, Brenda Randolph at *Africa Access,* our Social Studies Supervisor Barbara Graves, the Nigerian embassy, and Joanne at the Library of Congress.

Benchmark Books
Marshall Cavendish Corporation
99 White Plains Road
Tarrytown, New York 10591-9001

© Marshall Cavendish Corporation 1996

Library of Congress Cataloging-in-Publication Data

Adeeb, Hassan, date.
    Nigeria / by Hassan Adeeb and Bonnetta Adeeb.
        p.   cm. — (Exploring cultures of the world)
    Includes bibliographical references.
    Summary: Reviews the geography, history, people, customs, and the arts of the West African country of Nigeria.
    ISBN 0-7614-0190-3
    1. Nigeria—Juvenile literature. [1. Nigeria.] I. Adeeb, Bonnetta,   date.   II. Title.
III. Series.
    DT515.22.A34   1996
    966.9—dc20   95-15337

Printed and bound in Italy

Book design by Carol Matsuyama
Photo research by Debbie Needleman

Front cover: Nigerian villagers
Back cover: The Niger River

Photo Credits

Front cover and title page: courtesy of The Hutchison Library; back cover and page 10: courtesy of Victor Englebert; pages 6, 15: Tropix Photographic Library / D. Davis; pages 9, 32, 34, 54: The Hutchison Library; pages 11, 29, 36: Tropix Photographic Library / R. Cansdale; pages 13, 14, 50: Werner Forman / Art Resource, NY; page 19: Barbara Hakim; pages 21, 22, 45, 46: Jason Lauré; pages 24, 26: Robert Frerck / Odyssey Productions / Hillstrom Stock Photo; pages 30, 40, 43: Panos Pictures / Betty Press; page 31: Panos Pictures / Bruce Paton; pages 39, 48: The Hutchison Library / Sarah Errington; page 47: Mike Blake / Reuters / Bettmann; pages 52, 56: Panos Pictures / James Morris

Contents

A Hausa stands in front of his home on the hot and dusty Mambilla Plateau of northern Nigeria. It is easy to see why the Hausas trace their ancestors back to a hero who protected the source of water.

1
GEOGRAPHY AND HISTORY

Land of Contrasts, Land of Change

The Legend of Sarki the Snake

*V*oices boomed from the throne room. The sultan of Baghdad and his son, Prince Abu Yazid (AH-buh yah-ZEED), were having another bitter argument. Suddenly the doors burst open. The prince mounted his horse and raced out into the desert. He was leaving home—this time forever. Freed from his father's rule, Abu Yazid was now a prince without a kingdom.

Like a streak of lightning, Abu Yazid bolted south, across the Arabian Desert. After a long journey he entered the land of Kanem (KAH-nem), in western Africa. There he took shelter at the grand palace of the king. He remained for some months and eventually married the beautiful Kanem princess Maqira Daud (DAH-ood).

Abu Yazid's charm and understanding of trade brought him great riches and power. But as time passed, the king of Kanem grew jealous of the prince's wealth and began to plot against his life. Abu Yazid was forced to leave. Frightened and alone, he fled westward, while his pregnant wife remained behind. For protection, the prince sought out the smiths in the town of Gaya, who were known to work magic with iron. Then, armed with a special sword forged by the Gaya ironsmiths, he continued his journey.

Coming upon the town of Daura (DAH-uh-rah), Abu Yazid learned about Sarki, a monstrous snake that lived in the town well. The evil Sarki allowed the townspeople to draw precious water from the well only one day a week. Determined to slay the serpent, Abu Yazid waited for darkness, then approached the well. Sarki rose from the waters, as tall as two men, and fixed his angry red eyes upon the young man. As the great snake bent toward him, the fearless prince plunged his magic sword into its thick flesh. Sarki's bleeding head crashed to the ground.

The joyous people of Daura brought the news of Sarki's death to their queen, Dauranama. She promised half the town to whoever had slain the monster. Many came forward claiming they had killed Sarki. "Where is the head then?" asked the queen. "If you cannot produce the head, you are lying."

Finally Abu Yazid stood before the queen and pulled the huge serpent's head from his saddlebag. Impressed by the young man's courage, the queen did better than her promise. She married the prince, and they ruled Daura together. Abu Yazid became known as Markas Sarki—"Slayer of the Snake." In time, he was simply called Sarki.

Sarki and Queen Dauranama lived happily for many years. They had one son, who in turn had three sets of twins. Legend says that these six grandchildren, along with Abu Yazid's son by his first wife, became the founders of the seven states of the Hausa (HOW–suh) people of northern Nigeria. And in the language of the Hausa, the prince's legend lives on in the word for "king," sarki.

A Land Between Two "Seas"

The modern nation of Nigeria is on the coast of West Africa, with the Sahara Desert to its north, the Atlantic Ocean to its south. Nigeria covers over 356,000 square miles (930,000 square kilometers)—more than twice the size of California.

Within its borders, its lands differ widely from region to region.

If you rode down from Nigeria's northern border, you would first cross the dry, sandy lands where the Sahara Desert ends. This region is known as the Sahel (sah-HEHL), from the Arab word for "shore." Hundreds of years ago Arab traders led camel caravans south across the Sahara to exchange goods with the people of West Africa. To these merchants, crossing the desert was like navigating a vast, dry sea. When at last they reached the Sahara's southern fringe, they rested on the "shore."

South of the Sahel, tan, slender antelopes and gazelles feed on the grasslands of Nigeria's savanna. The gently rolling

As in ancient times, the people of West Africa still cross the vast Sahara Desert by camel caravan.

grasslands are like large open parks dotted by baobab (BOW-bab) trees and gingerbread palms. Herds of wildebeest roam the savanna, quickly scattering when hyenas, lions, or leopards lunge from the brush.

In the center of Nigeria is the Jos Plateau. High, flat, and grassy, the plateau has a cool, pleasant climate throughout the year. South of the Jos Plateau the Niger and Benue Rivers meet, dividing Nigeria's northern highlands from the lowlands of the south.

The Niger is the most important river of West Africa, flowing east 2,600 miles (4,180 kilometers) from the highlands of the Republic of Guinea. Crocodiles live in the Niger River, and occasionally a hippopotamus will overturn people's canoes or boats. The Niger turns south after meeting the Benue River and flows through the center of Nigeria's tropical rain forest.

The life-giving Niger River is a peaceful route for transporting goods across West Africa.

As in other areas of the world, much of the valuable rain forest is being cut down to make way for farms and to provide lumber for buildings, furniture, and boats.

Near Nigeria's southern border, the Niger breaks up into a maze of small rivers, creeks, and swampy lagoons. Here the fresh water of the river meets the salt water of the sea. This region's fertile plain, formed by soil deposited by the river and fed by its fresh waters, is known as the Niger Delta.

A shallow stream makes a good spot for washing laundry in Nigeria's lush rain forest.

It rains nearly every day in the delta region. The air is heavy and moist. Monkeys and chimpanzees squeak and chatter in high tree branches. Parrots, hawks, and red-winged touraco birds fly across marshy swamps. (Many of these creatures are threatened by the construction of oil derricks and pumps in the petroleum-rich Niger Delta.) Manatees swim among the tangled roots of mangrove trees—European sailors once thought these gentle, fishlike animals were mermaids. The dense mangrove forests protect Nigeria's shoreline from being worn away by crashing ocean waves.

West of the delta, along the coast of the Bight of Benin, a bay off the Atlantic Ocean, are white, sandy beaches. Here the leaves of tall coconut and raffia palm trees blow and rustle in the constant ocean breezes.

Nigeria lies near the equator, and its year-round temperatures range from 65°F to 95°F (18°C to 35°C). Northern Nigeria is dry and hot; southern Nigeria is wet and steamy. There are two seasons—a rainy season, from April to October, and a dry season, from November to March. During the rainy season southern Nigeria is pounded with a seemingly endless downpour. But between December and March, strong, dusty *harmattan* winds blow off the Sahara Desert, lowering temperatures and humidity throughout the land.

Ancient Nigeria

Although the nation of Nigeria is young, people have been living in this region of West Africa since the Stone Age. Those early people hunted, farmed, and herded sheep, cattle, and goats. In time a sophisticated society developed near the northern town of Nok. Evidence of the Nok culture was first uncovered in 1943, when the head of a terra-cotta (clay) sculpture was found in the rubble of a tin mine. When other terra-cotta heads were discovered, historians began to wonder if these sculptures came from an unknown civilization. Today they believe that the Nok clay figures were created by a group of people who lived between 300 B.C. and A.D. 200. These ancient people were farmers and skilled ironworkers as well as talented sculptors.

Clay sculptures discovered at Nok, in northern Nigeria, let us look back two thousand years to an ancient civilization.

The Early States

Between A.D. 1100 and 1400, a number of important states arose within Nigeria. Southwest of the Niger River, deep in the rain forests, the Yoruba (YAW-ruh-buh) people built large cities, including Ife (EE-fay) and Benin (be-NEEN). Ancient Ife was surrounded by thick mud walls. Streets and walkways had decorative patterns made from pieces of broken pottery and white quartz pebbles. In the center of the city stood the large palace of the Ife king, or *oni*. The *onis* imported copper, from which artists created magnificent bronze and copper statues.

This sixteenth- to seventeenth-century bronze plaque of a well-armed king decorated the palace at the Yoruba city of Benin.

These beautiful statues show the swords, helmets, jewelry, and royal clothing of the Yorubas' ancient *onis*.

In the forests east of the Niger Delta the Ibo (EE-boh) people farmed yams. The Ibo lived in small villages, each governed by a council of elders. Village government was democratic. All people were free to speak at council meetings, but men with special abilities, wealth, or wisdom enjoyed the greatest respect and influence.

In northern Nigeria the savannas were home to the wandering Fulani (foo-LAHN-ee) people and to the states of Kanem-Bornu and Hausa. The rulers, or *mais*, of Kanem-Bornu expanded their empire through conquest. The best known of

Hausa men in traditional costumes guard the palace of their emir, or ruler, in the ancient city of Kano.

Bornu's *mais* was Idris Alooma. In the sixteenth century, when Kanem-Bornu was threatened by the fierce Tuareg (TWAH-reg)—blue-veiled, camel-riding warriors from the desert— Idris Alooma defended his empire by equipping his army with muskets from Turkey.

West of Kanem-Bornu the Hausa people built up seven independent city-states. The seven states of the Hausa empire often fought one another for control of trade with the Arab merchants who crossed the Sahara Desert from North Africa. But the hostility among the Hausa states cooled as Islam, the religion of these Arab traders, began to spread across northern Nigeria.

Invaders from the Sea

Ever since the 1400s European merchants had been sailing to West Africa to trade metal tools, cooking utensils, cloth, and glassware for Africa's gold, ivory, and spices. In 1480 the Europeans began to trade their goods for a much more valuable commodity: slaves. European colonies in North and South America needed workers for sugar, rice, indigo, cotton, and tobacco plantations. Africans sold fellow Africans to the Europeans to work as slaves on the plantations in the Americas.

Most Africans sold into the Atlantic slave trade were prisoners of war, debtors, criminals, or victims of religious punishment. Most were young adults. Between the fifteenth and early nineteenth centuries the slave trade robbed West Africa of twenty million to thirty million young men and women. Many thousands died on the long trek to the West African coast or on the foul and cramped journey across the Atlantic Ocean.

Why did Africans sell their own people into slavery?

People did not see themselves as "Africans" but as members of their own ethnic groups. Just as in Europe the French consider the Germans members of a separate nationality, the Yorubas of West Africa considered the Hausa a different people. And when the Yoruba defeated the Hausa in battle, they

THE WARRIOR QUEEN

While most of the Hausa states were ruled by men, the state of Zaria had several women rulers. Princess Amina became queen of Zaria in 1576. Amina never married. For her, making war was more interesting than being a wife and mother. Amina commanded her troops in battle, and over a period of thirty-four years, her armies won victory after victory.

sold their Hausa prisoners of war to the Europeans as slaves.

In the early nineteenth century the British, who were the largest slave traders, made it illegal to sell slaves to the United States. The British had lost their North American colonies, and they now believed that African labor could produce more profit for British businesses on the African continent. British explorers had learned that Africa was rich in natural resources—materials that could be used to fuel the growing Industrial Revolution. Timber, gum, gold, ivory, and palm oil were abundant in the Niger Delta. The British wanted to control the trade of these goods, especially the lucrative palm oil trade. Palm oil was in great demand for use in soap, candles, and other products.

Along with France, Belgium, Portugal, and Germany, Britain began to divide up the continent of Africa like a pie. For twenty years the people of Nigeria and other African regions resisted the Europeans. But by the beginning of the twentieth century all resistance had been defeated, and Nigeria became a British colony.

British Rule

The British organized the building of roads, railroads, and harbors throughout Nigeria. It became easier to move raw materials and crops to the coast for shipment to England and to move goods made in England to the Nigerian interior. Trade during the colonial era brought wealth to many British businesspeople.

The new roads and railroads also brought British missionaries to Nigeria. Missionaries converted thousands of people to Christianity. They also taught Nigerians the English language.

Many Nigerians resisted British control. In 1929 some Nigerian marketwomen were shot and killed in the city of Aba when they attacked court buildings and factories. They were protesting the low prices British merchants paid for their goods. Other Nigerians tried nonviolent tactics to end British rule. Some became part of the Pan-African Movement. This organization of black people from the United States, Africa, and the Caribbean Islands believed that the best response to white racism was the creation of independent black nations in Africa and promoted independence for the people of Africa.

By the 1920s some Africans had begun to think of themselves not as Yoruba, Ibo, or Hausa but as Nigerian. These early nationalists had a vision of a united and independent Nigeria. They pointed out that Nigerians were forced to pay taxes to the British but were denied the right to vote in the colonial government. Herbert Macauley and other Nigerian nationalists formed the Nigerian National Democratic Party (NNDP) to fight this injustice. The NNDP pushed for reforms that

Millions of worshipers still practice the Christian faith brought to Nigeria by British missionaries during the colonial era.

would give Nigerians free public education and a greater voice in their government.

The Zikist movement, led by Dr. Nnamdi ("Zik") Azikiwe, believed that the NNDP was not forceful enough. The Zikists organized workers' boycotts and strikes. In 1949 twenty striking coal miners were shot and killed by colonial police. Riots and looting broke out and the British realized they were losing control. Finally, in 1960, Britain gave up colonial rule, and Nigeria became independent.

A Struggling New Nation

The first years of Nigerian independence were stormy. The country was divided into three major regions: the Northern Region, made up mostly of the Hausa people, the Western Region of the Yoruba, and the Eastern Region of the Ibo. The

NIGERIAN GOVERNMENT

In Nigeria, several traditional ways of governing exist side by side with the modern national government. The Ibo people are ruled by a council of village elders. This council is composed of the oldest men from the main families. The Yoruba people are governed by a king, or *oni*. From his palace in Benin, the *oni* makes decisions with the advice of the queen mother, royal nobles, and town chiefs. Among the Islamic people of the north, the Fulani are ruled by the sultan of Sokoto, and the Hausa are ruled by the emirs of Kano and Katsina.

Nigeria's national government is run by a military dictator. In 1993 the nation's minister of defense took over as president and head of state. According to law, the president must govern with the assistance of a thirty-three-member Executive Council, which he appoints. Nigeria is divided into thirty states, each administered by an elected governor. The highest court in the land is the Federal Supreme Court; the president appoints the chief justice and up to fifteen federal judges.

three groups disagreed over who should have control of the nation's affairs. Outbreaks of violence occurred.

In 1966 a group of young army officers seized control of Nigeria's government. Many Nigerians hoped the military takeover would end the violence. But conflicts continued, especially in the oil-rich Eastern Region, where ten thousand Ibo people were attacked and killed.

The Ibo people broke away from Nigeria in 1967, forming a new nation called the Republic of Biafra (bee-AF-rah). For two and a half years Nigerian forces fought to win back the Biafran territories. In this tragic civil war over two million Nigerians died. Many people in Biafra starved to death. At last Biafra surrendered to the Nigerian federal government. The country was one nation again.

Though traditional rulers have no legal power in Nigeria today, they are still respected by the military government.

Nigeria's great oil wealth made it possible for the war-torn nation to be rebuilt and for education and health care to be improved. But the end of the civil war and these improvements did not bring unity. Conflicts among Nigeria's peoples continued, and life was made harder by the corruption of those in power. Today, Nigeria still has a military government. The nation continues to face the challenge of restoring civilian rule. Many Nigerians hope that one day soon they will be able to vote for their leaders in a free and democratic government.

A Hausa girl carries goods in an age-old way.

2
THE PEOPLE

The Many Faces of Nigeria

A Mix of Cultures

How many different ways do people say hello in Nigeria? *"Sannu"* is the way the Hausa people say hello. A Fulani girl might greet you by saying, *"Jungwali"* (jung-WAH-lee), and you could answer back with *"Umbalijam"* (uhm-bah-lee-JAHM). In the south a Yoruba person will greet you with *"Bawoni"* (bah-woh-NEE). Across the delta, the Ibos say *"Kedu"* (KEE-doo). People who practice the Islamic religion greet each other with *"Assalamu Alaikum"* (AH-sah-LAHM-uh ah-LAY-khum).

Nigeria is home to people with many different languages, histories, and customs. While nearly four hundred languages and dialects (regional varieties of the same language) are spoken, the four major languages are Ibo, Yoruba, Fulani, and Hausa. When Nigerians go to the bank or a government office, they use English, the nation's official language.

Many Ibo-speaking people live in small villages east of the Niger Delta and in the bustling southeastern cities of Port Harcourt and Calabar. During British colonial rule, the Ibos

A Fulani herder in need of a mount might visit this northern camel market.

attended British missionary schools. Many of these British-educated Ibos today are doctors, lawyers, businesspeople, and government workers. Their success has created tension between them and the peoples of the north and west.

The rain forests and savannas of southwest Nigeria are the traditional homeland of the Yoruba-speaking people. Many Yorubas today live in towns and cities. They often continue the traditional Yoruba religious practices, worshiping hundreds of gods and other spirits.

Nigeria's tall, slender, straight-haired Fulani-speaking people live mostly in the nation's north. Dressed in long, billowy robes, camel-riding Fulani herders graze their red-brown zebu cattle across the grassy savanna. These Fulani herding families are nomadic. Every few days they pack up

SAY IT IN . . .

Many languages and dialects are used in Nigeria. Here is a comparison of some of the same words in English and four of the major Nigerian language groups:

English	Fulani	Hausa	Ibo	Yoruba
I'm fine	Jam tan (JAM-taan)	Kalau (KA-lay-U)	Adimnma (ah-DEE-mm-NMAA)	A dupe (ah DEW-pay)
one	goqo (GO-quo)	daya (DA-ya)	otu (o-TWO)	eni (EE-nee)
two	didi (DEE-dee)	biyu (BEE-you)	abua (ah-BOO-ah)	eji (EE-gee)
three	tati (TA-tea)	uku (OO-coo)	ato (ah-TOE)	eta (EE-ta)
nine	jeenayi (gee-NA-yee)	tara (TAA-ra)	iteghete (IT-egg-HE-tea)	esan (EE-san)
ten	sappo (SAP-poe)	goma (GO-ma)	iri (EE-ree)	ewa (EE-wa)

their animal-hide tents and seek fresh pastures for their cattle, camels, goats, and sheep. Other Fulanis are farmers. They live in small villages and towns, growing crops such as guinea corn, millet, and rice.

Also living in northern Nigeria are the Hausa-speaking people. The Hausa people weave cloth with detailed, colorfully embroidered patterns. They design dyed leather saddles for camels and horses. Hausa merchants trade their goods all over West Africa.

*At a dye pit in the northern city of Kano, a craftsman makes beautiful
tie-dyed cloth.*

Faith and Worship

Nigerians are a deeply religious people. Most believe that one supreme god created the heavens and earth. Many also believe that lesser gods live in natural elements such as rain and thunder. Some of these lesser gods are mischievous, while others are good.

In Yoruba society women are greatly respected as religious leaders and priestesses. The Yorubas worship not only their gods but also the spirits of their ancestors. Through offerings and sacrifices, they call on their ancestors' powers to help them in their daily lives.

Like the Yorubas, the Ibo people once worshiped many spirits and gods. But today most Ibos practice Christianity, and little is remembered of the traditional Ibo religion.

About half the people of Nigeria practice the religion of Islam. Islamic people follow the teachings of the prophet Muhammad. They wear clothes that cover the entire body, they do not eat pork, and they call God by the name Allah. In many trading towns people practice both Islam and their traditional religion.

In fact, across Nigeria few people of any faith would ever show disrespect to their traditional beliefs. An Islamic Fulani farmer praying for rain might say his Islamic prayers, then sacrifice a chicken to the river god just to be sure. Some churches in Nigeria blend Christianity with traditional African religious beliefs.

Life in the Countryside

What is it like to live and work in the Nigerian countryside? The people of rural Nigeria earn their living in many different ways. In the thousands of small villages on riverbanks, the savanna,

IFE: WHERE THE WORLD BEGAN

According to a legend of the Yoruba people, the world began when the god Oduduwa came down from heaven on a chain. Oduduwa carried a cockerel (a male chicken), one palm nut, and the shell of a calabash (a gourd) containing soil. He threw the soil down onto the endless sea, causing land to appear. The cockerel dug a hole in the land, and the god planted the palm nut, creating earth's vegetation. This place where the world began was named Ife, and Oduduwa became its first *oni*, or ruler. Later Oduduwa sent his sixteen sons out from Ife to begin other Yoruba kingdoms. Today Ife remains an important city to the Yoruba people.

and in the rain forest, farming has long been the most important occupation. Nigeria's farmers tend fields of maize, cassavas (starchy plants, similar to sweet potatoes), yams, and rice. In some areas farmers grow bananas, pineapples, and cocoyams, which look like giant potatoes. Along the Niger and Benue Rivers fishermen catch giant one-hundred-pound (45 kilograms) perch in strong nets. In the north many Nigerians herd cattle, sheep, and goats. Rural Nigerians also work as teachers, veterinarians, merchants, laborers, and postal workers. Others spin, weave, and dye cloth.

Where two major country roads cross, you will often find women selling fresh fruits and vegetables and sharing the latest news. At these country crossroads, handmade goods such as cloth and pottery also may be sold. Before the sun sets, the marketwomen gather up their baskets, count their profits, and head for home.

Family homes, or compounds, in Nigeria's countryside are made up of separate houses for each adult member of the

Village women work together to pound seeds into flour.

family. These houses are surrounded by walls, which create an open courtyard. Much of the family's daily activity occurs in this open-air "room."

Many compounds are built of cement or brick. In the dry Sahel and the savanna, they may be constructed from fired mud brick; in forest areas, wood and palm leaves often are used. Compound walls sometimes are painted with bright geometric designs.

The Big Cities

Nigeria is home to two of Africa's largest cities, Lagos (LAH-gohs) and Ibadan (EE-bah-dahn). Over ten million people fill the southwestern port city of Lagos, the nation's former capital. The streets of Lagos teem with cars, cabs, mammywagons (colorfully painted trucks or vans), street vendors, and people from all over the world. Ibadan, located in the middle of the rich agricultural region of southwestern Nigeria, is a center of trade, education, and industry.

In Port Harcourt, another bustling southern city, dock-workers load sacks of peanuts and cocoa beans onto ships bound for locations around the world. People from all over West Africa come to Port Harcourt and other port cities to set up streetside stands. There they sell fruit, drinks, tasty stews, and any other items that might help them earn a living.

A beautiful new capital was built in the center of the nation, at Abuja (ah-BOO-jah), in 1991. To the north of the capital lies the ancient Hausa city of Kano, famous for its traditional adobe (sun-dried brick) architecture. Kano's streets are filled with merchants selling traditional woven blankets, colorfully dyed leather, baskets, and delicate jewelry.

Cocoa beans from the rain forest pass through Nigeria's port cities to chocolate-processing factories around the world.

In recent years many Nigerians have moved to the cities, seeking good-paying jobs and a better future. A shortage of affordable housing for all these new residents has caused many problems.

Modern offices, banks, and skyscrapers loom over the shantytowns of Nigeria's homeless city people. The shantytowns' flimsy shacks have no electricity or running water, and poor sanitation spreads disease. The rapid growth of cities also has increased crime. Traffic jams make moving through Nigeria's busy cities a daily challenge.

A crowded street in Lagos shows why Nigerians call their traffic jams "go slows."

A Nigerian family may include a father, two or more wives, and many children.

3

FAMILY LIFE, FESTIVALS, AND FOOD

In Homes and Hearts

The Nigerian Family

Nafise is eight and her brother Ibrahim is ten. They live with their parents and the rest of their family in a Yoruba village outside the city of Abuja. Nafise and Ibrahim have twelve brothers and sisters. There are so many children in the family because their father has three wives. Although each wife has her own private living quarters, the three women work together to care for all the children. Whenever a child gets hurt or is sad, there is always someone close by to give comfort.

Nafise and Ibrahim's father has many responsibilities. He takes care of a large family with wives, children, aging parents, and other relatives. Only responsible Nigerian men can have more than one wife. They must be able to support their wives and children, and they must ask for the permission of their first wife to marry again. If a man does not properly care for his wife, her relatives will take her back, causing him great embarrassment.

Nafise and Ibrahim's mother works with the other wives to care for the children and home, prepare meals, and raise vegetables such as okra, squash, peppers, pumpkins, tomatoes, onions, and black-eyed peas.

Like many Nigerian children, Nafise and Ibrahim live in a compound of several houses, which they share with their extended family—brothers and sisters, parents, grandparents, aunts, uncles, and cousins. Besides all these relatives, the compound is often filled with friends of the family, who come to talk and laugh together. The men chew on bitter red kola nuts;

The three women in red-and-white dresses are married to the man in the window. Wives of the same husband often dress alike.

the juice from the kola nut is an ingredient in Coca-Cola and other soft drinks enjoyed around the world.

Today most of the talk in Nafise and Ibrahim's compound is about their cousin Flora, who is getting married soon. Each ethnic group in Nigeria has its own special way of celebrating a marriage. In most societies the groom gives the bride's family a "bride price." This payment of money, livestock, or other valuable property is a sign of the groom's appreciation of the value the young woman has to her family.

When Flora marries, she will move to the city, and in time Nafise may join her. Young girls from the village sometimes move to the city to help their married cousins or sisters take care of their children and households. The older sister or cousin repays the younger girl by helping to pay for her education.

While many young people today are moving to the cities in hopes of earning more money, strong ties to the village remain. Family members who have done well in the city often are expected to support and educate less fortunate relatives back home. Sometimes very wealthy city dwellers may even support their entire village.

The Place of the Children

All the children of Nafise and Ibrahim's family live, play, and work together in the family compound. Nafise and Ibrahim's chores include helping their mother tend the garden. Nafise sells vegetables and live chickens on market days. Ibrahim works beside his father, weeding the cocoyam fields. Doing homework is another very important responsibility.

After the evening meal all the children sit in the family courtyard, at their grandfather's feet. Under the moonlit sky they learn songs, proverbs, and fables. In this way tales of

Giving baby brother a bath is one of this Nigerian boy's chores.

legendary heroes like Sarki are passed down from one generation to another.

Celebrating Life

Nigerian festivals are joyous celebrations. Ancient stories are acted out in poetry, music, and dance. The people wear colorful costumes and masks. Many festivals take place during spring and in the harvest season. The Ibos celebrate when the first yams are ready to eat. Other groups hold festivals to honor a new chief

NIGERIAN PROVERBS

He who is being carried on another's back
does not realize how far the town is.

Before healing others, heal yourself.

The bird flies high, but always returns to earth.

Children of the same mother do not always agree.

Before shooting, one must aim.

When the mouse laughs at the cat, there is a hole nearby.

Fine words do not produce food.

Seeing is better than hearing.

or to recognize a relative who has died and become an ancestor spirit. Nigerians in the north hold horseback-riding competitions after Ramadan (RAH-muh-dahn), the thirty-day Islamic period of fasting from dawn to sunset.

The Gelede (je-LE-day) festival is one of the most important celebrations of the Yoruba people. Held before the spring rainy season, Gelede honors women as symbols of nature and earth's fertility. The highlight of the festival is a grand parade of musicians and dancers wearing brilliantly colored costumes and masks. People come from all around the world to witness this spectacular event.

In northern Nigeria the end of the growing season is the time for the Argungun (AHR-goon-goon) Fishing Festival. Over five thousand men celebrate by swimming and diving in a mile-long section of the Sokoto River. With butterfly-shaped fishing nets, they pull huge, silvery Niger perch out of the splashing waters. There are also exciting canoe races and diving tournaments.

Honoring the Dead

Like festivals, Nigerian funerals are a time for the gathering of family, friends, and community. Shortly after a person dies, he or she is buried. But the ceremonies honoring the person last for weeks and even months.

To Nigerians death is not an end but a journey into a spiritual world. In elaborate ceremonies filled with music and dancing, the dead person is given the status of an ancestor. The spirits of the ancestors are believed to guide the actions of living people. The Ibos believe that the soul of a dead person is brought back to life in a new body.

Dressing Up

Proud-looking Nigerian men stroll through village and city streets wearing *abas*, cloaks that might be used as a blanket or an overcoat. Some men also wear a flowing cotton or silk gown known as an *agbada*. The gown is worn with pants made of matching material. A man's wealth can be judged by the number of layers in his *agbada*. Fulani men wear long embroidered robes with baggy silk or cotton drawstring trousers. On their heads they wear a fez—a brimless flat-topped hat—or a close-fitting skullcap. But in the cities many men put aside their traditional clothing and wear modern suits, shirts, and neckties.

Many Nigerian women wear a vibrantly colored flowing gown called a *boubou*. The more fashionable *boubous* have several pieces: a short blouse, a wrapper that covers the woman from waist to ankles, and a matching shawl that drapes over the shoulders and wraps around the waist. A narrower wrapper tied on the head can also be used as a veil.

Women in the north who belong to the Islamic faith often

Clothing adds to the color and excitement of a Nigerian festival.

wear dark colors that cover their whole bodies. Fulani women favor the color red, which they accent with beautiful gold and amber jewelry.

Uniformed schoolchildren gather in the doorway of their classroom in the city of Kaduna, central Nigeria.

4

SCHOOL AND RECREATION

Proud Traditions, New Dreams

A Day in School

Like many Nigerian children who live in the countryside, Ibrahim and Nafise awake to the crow of roosters. They feed the chickens and hogs, and eat a breakfast of fruit and garri (toasted cassava flour). Then the children set off on their walk down the dirt road that leads to the village school. On the way to school, they cross small creeks, spot colorful peacocks, and hear the calls of tropical birds and monkeys in the trees above them.

Ibrahim and his friends kick around a soccer ball before school starts. Nafise joins the other girls in a clapping game called *tente* (ten-TAY). When the school drums sound, the children leave their games to line up and enter their small tin-roofed school.

Together all the schoolchildren sing Nigeria's national anthem, then say a prayer of hope for the nation. Taking their seats, they begin to recite a traditional poem of their people. Nafise and Ibrahim read from books written in their native language, Yoruba. They practice math and handwriting, and study the English language. When the drums sound again for recess, they run outside to play. After the break they return for their daily science and history lessons. Finally, at one o'clock, the dismissal drums send all the hungry students scurrying home to lunch.

Modern Education

Education is very important in Nigeria. Some students, like Ibrahim and Nafise, attend government schools, which are free. Others go to private schools. There are also two kinds of religious schools—Koranic (KHOR-ahn-ik) schools for Islamic children and Christian missionary schools.

No matter what type of school they attend, all Nigerian schoolchildren wear a uniform. For girls the uniform is a blouse and jumper or skirt, for boys a shirt and shorts. All children must study the same basic subjects: math, reading, science, handwriting, and language.

School buildings are different in the city and countryside. Students in Nigeria's rural areas attend classes in small one-room schools or sometimes under the shade of a large baobab tree. Classes in the city are more likely to be held in a modern building.

Most schools in Nigeria do not have enough books, maps, or science equipment. Like many inner-city schools in the United States, they also are overcrowded. The Nigerian government is trying to correct this problem by building more free public schools. But even overcrowded schools are a sign of progress: In the past many Nigerian children were unable to attend school because their parents needed them at home. Now, however, they are required to graduate from senior secondary school, or high school. Attendance has increased

A young student at an Islamic school recites from the holy book the Koran.

markedly since the new requirements began. Today nearly four million Nigerian students attend government-run secondary schools.

Universities and vocational schools prepare young people for jobs. The Universities of Ibadan and Lagos have educated many young Nigerian scientists, engineers, writers, and doctors. Vocational schools train students to work as skilled farmers, plumbers, mechanics, and electricians. After graduating from college or vocational school, young people are required to join the National Youth Service Corps for one year. In the service they may become teachers or work on medical, forestry, or agricultural projects outside their native state. The service, which gives young Nigerians the opportunity to learn about other regions, promotes understanding among Nigeria's different peoples.

Keeping the Old Ways

Some Nigerian children attend traditional schools in the bush, or forest, where they learn the history and customs of their people. Ten- to fourteen-year-old boys may be taken from their compounds to a special schoolhouse in the bush. There they will live for a time, joining in hunting and sporting activities designed to teach them courage and endurance. Boys from northern herding families learn to take care of camels, horses, and goats. Some young men are taught a special trade, such as weaving textiles, making leather saddles, or forging tools and weapons in an iron furnace.

Traditional schools in the bush teach girls about the responsibilities of being a wife and mother. Girls also learn the skills of weaving, pottery, and herbal medicine. Sometimes parents in the city send their daughters back home to the family village to learn the ways and beliefs of their people.

At the completion of bush school, a young person's cheeks are cut in two or three places. These permanent marks are a sign that the child has entered adulthood.

Fun for Young and Old

If you can dig eight holes in the ground and find thirty-two small pebbles, you can play *ayu*. People all over West Africa play *ayu*, although in some nations the popular game is called *warri* or *mankala*. Played with smooth pebbles, beans, or seeds that are moved across rows of holes in a board, rock, or the ground, *ayu* is similar to checkers or backgammon. Nearly everyone in Nigeria, from small children to old men, enjoy sitting in the shade of a baobab tree, laughing and plotting their winning *ayu* moves.

In the villages children don't have modern games, but like children everywhere, they know how to have fun. They play the same games their parents and grandparents played, with toys made from plants and other natural objects. Girls

The scars on this proud young woman's cheeks tell the world she has completed bush school.

play with doll babies, and enjoy singing and clapping games. Boys play games that teach endurance and bravery. In the big cities children like to watch television, but electricity has not yet reached all the rural areas.

In northern Nigeria horseback riding and camel and horse racing are popular sports. In the delta region pounding drums keep the rhythm as oarsmen row in fiercely competitive boat and canoe races. All across Nigeria boxing and wrestling matches always draw large crowds. Sometimes the excited fans even start punching each other! Boxers and wrestlers

Riders show off their skills during the Sallah celebration honoring the sultan of the city of Sokoto.

from small villages and towns train for years to win state, national, and international championships.

The British introduced the sports of tennis, rugby, polo, golf, and cricket into Nigeria, and these are still favorites among wealthy Nigerians. Another sport made popular by the British is soccer, which the Nigerians call football.

The national soccer team brought pride and honor to Nigeria in the 1994 World Cup competition. People from all regions and ethnic groups watched on television and cheered as their heroes rose to the semifinal rounds. It was the strongest performance yet by an African soccer team. Nigeria's athletes also have made constant progress in other sports competitions, such as the All-African Games, the British Commonwealth Games, and the Olympics.

In the past Nigerian girls were not allowed to participate in organized sports, but today women's teams are being organized across the country. In 1991 Nigeria's Mary Onyali proved herself the fastest woman sprinter in competition in Africa. At

Nigeria's relay team, including Mary Onyali (far right), rejoices after winning the bronze medal at the 1992 Summer Olympics.

first Mary's father had not wanted her to run track, but after she won a track scholarship to a college in the United States, he changed his opinion. New attitudes about women in sports are allowing Nigerian girls of all ages to stretch their horizons.

FAMOUS ATHLETES FROM NIGERIA

Hogan "Kid" Bassey, 1957–1959 world featherweight boxing champion

Peter Konyegwachie, 1984 winner of Olympic silver medal for boxing

Mary Onyali, 1991 fastest woman sprinter in Africa

Rasheed Yekini, 1994 World Cup leading soccer scorer

Samson Siasia, 1994 World Cup soccer forward

Akeem Olajuwon, center for professional basketball's Houston Rockets

Christian Okoye, member of the Kansas City Chiefs professional football team

During a festival honoring the Yoruba god Ogun, an elaborate costume transforms a dancer into a work of art.

5
THE ARTS

Beauty All Around

Why do Nigerian festival dancers wear masks? They are following an age-old tradition in which masks represent forces of nature, gods, or ancestor spirits. While wearing their masks, festival dancers move to the drumbeat and act out stories of old. Many Nigerians believe that during these performances, a real force or spirit enters the dancers' costumes. During the magical time of festivals, these masked spirits get a chance to come out and play.

Most African festival masks are carved from wood and cover the performer's entire body with layers of raffia grass or bright colorful cloth. Though they are valued by art collectors, masks are not made to be hung on a wall or displayed in a museum. Like all forms of Nigerian art, they are meant to be used.

Nigerians express their sense of beauty in practical, everyday objects, including items such as furniture and clothing. Each village, town, and ethnic group decorates its objects of art with its own special symbols and designs. These pictures of animals, religious symbols, and geometric patterns adorn the simplest pots and gourds. Even spoons or hair combs may be highly decorated in modern or ancient patterns.

This wooden mask was made in the twentieth century and worn by festival dancers in southeastern Nigeria.

Images from the Past

The Nok sculptures, dating back more than two thousand years, are among the oldest-known terra-cotta sculptures in Africa. These sophisticated clay figures are evidence of the fine craftsmanship of the artists who created them.

The people of the ancient Yoruba cities of Ife and Benin also were gifted sculptors. From Ife came intricate figures in terra-cotta and bronze. Benin's artists created bronze, ivory, and wooden figures, masks, and plaques that are prized today for their beauty and detail. Some of the Benin statues are images of the kings and queens of that ancient kingdom. Others are door plaques showing important events in Nigerian history. The sculptures of the Nok, Benin, and Ife peoples give us a picture of what life was like in ancient Nigeria.

Oral Traditions and Modern Tales

In Nigeria myths, fables, histories, poems, riddles, and songs are passed down in spoken form from generation to generation. This is known as an oral tradition. For thousands of years—before the development of writing—it was the only way people learned about their past. Today Nigerian expression is a rich blend of old and new, with modern writers working alongside storytellers called griots (GREE-ohs). These men and women memorize and recite tales of the lives and deeds of past kings, villages, and towns.

Several of Nigeria's modern writers have become famous around the world. Wole Soyinka (WOH-le shaw-YIN-kah), a Nigerian poet, playwright, and novelist, was the first African to win the Nobel Prize in literature. Soyinka writes stories about the tensions between old traditions and modern lifestyles.

Flora Nwapa was the first Nigerian woman to have a

THE ART IN CRAFTS

Nigerians express their artistry and appreciation of beauty in many traditional crafts and industries.

Textiles. Spinning, weaving, and dying cloth are all traditional industries. Textiles from northern Nigeria are sold all over the world.

Pottery. Making clay plates, bowls, and pots is a traditional industry for women. While the pottery is still wet, designs are carved onto the surface. Clay pottery is sun-dried and then fired at high temperatures.

Metalworking. Smiths in Nigeria have been working in iron, tin, copper, and gold for centuries. Iron ore traditionally was smelted at high temperatures in clay furnaces. While red-hot, the soft iron was hammered into axes, knives, swords, and farm tools.

Leather working. After the Europeans arrived in Nigeria, soft leather made from the red goats of Sokoto was exported through North Africa to Europe. There it was mistakenly named Moroccan leather, after the North African country Morocco.

Weaving textiles is a traditional and honored craft.

novel published. Nwapa has written many stories for young people, and she owns a company that publishes Nigerian folk-tales for children.

The young Nigerian author Ben Okri writes short stories and novels that weave together modern themes and traditional beliefs. In Okri's tales the spirits of those who have died and those not yet born influence the lives of modern-day people.

Chinua Achebe (CHIN-wah uh-CHAY-bay) is today's most widely read Nigerian writer. In Achebe's stories and books for children, the characters are animals such as the spider, monkey, turtle, and lion. Achebe's novel *Things Fall Apart* has been translated into forty languages and has inspired a Nigerian television series.

A Musical Mix

Inside the Sounds

If you visited Nigeria, you would hear the sounds of music wherever you went. Nigerians use music to express emotions, to communicate across long distances, and to get in touch with the spirit world. There are songs for war, songs for the hunt, songs for work and play. No festival or celebration is complete without music.

The high and low tones of Nigerian music make instruments "talk," or express feelings. Rhythm—music's repeating pattern or beat—is also an important part of African musical expression. The pulsing rhythm set by the drums gets people dancing and helps them join the musicians on a "journey" to the spirit world. Another familiar element of African music is call and response. The lead singer, drummer, or horn player of a musical group plays a melody, and the rest of the group repeats it or responds to it.

African drums of different shapes and sizes produce a great variety of sounds.

Many types of instruments play a part in the traditional music of Nigeria, but drums are the most important. Made from the stretched hide of cattle or antelope, drums may be elaborately decorated or even dressed in ceremonial cloth. They vary in size, from a few inches to eight feet high (2.5 meters), and may be played by hand or with sticks. The unique squeeze drum has strings running along its sides; the drum is squeezed under the drummer's arm to create a full range of sounds.

Traditional Nigerian vibrating instruments such as clappers, rattles, and bells are shaken or struck to help drummers carry the beat. Wind instruments such as pipes and whistles are made from bamboo or from cow or antelope horns. In the north the Hausa and Fulani peoples play simple fiddles, flutes, horns, xylophones, water drums, and lutes. The lute, a pear-shaped string instrument, is plucked, strummed, or bowed to create a variety of sounds. Singing and clapping also are basic "instruments" of northern music.

The Modern Beat

Highlife, sometimes called guitar pop, began in West Africa during the 1920s. This popular style of music combines traditional West African rhythms with modern European instruments such as saxophones, clarinets, brass trumpets, pianos, and guitars.

In the 1940s a Nigerian band led by King Sunny Ade (ah-DAY) popularized the music called *juju*. The crooning vocals, piercing guitars, and driving drums of *juju* music combine musical traditions from both the Christian and Yoruba religions. *Juju* also was influenced by the music of former slaves returning to Nigeria after slavery ended in Brazil in 1888.

In the 1970s Nigerian musician and songwriter Fela Randome Anikopo Kuti became an international superstar. Fela's songs about injustice are cherished by many young people seeking change, both in Africa and the United States.

Today Nigerians enjoy both traditional African music and new sounds from all over the world. Pop, jazz, rap, and the reggae music of the Caribbean are all popular in Nigeria. African-American performers such as Michael Jackson and African stars such as Angelique Kito, Salif Keita, and Lucky Dube sell millions of recordings in Nigeria.

Dancing to Life

Like music, dance is a part of everyday life in Nigeria. Dance is often included in festivals and religious and social ceremonies. Special dances are performed at weddings and funerals. Other dances are believed to ensure a successful hunt or

Today many Nigerian artists create modern works of art that reflect ancient forms of beauty.

plentiful rain for a good harvest. Some dances may only be performed by women or by men, and there are even dances that only royalty may perform. Children dance not only on special occasions but every day, just for fun.

Some Nigerian dances have very complex foot patterns and other movements. These elements of the dance are different for each ethnic group. For example, when young Fulani men who are looking for wives perform the playful Yaake (yah-ah-KEE) dance, they roll their painted eyes, turn their heads from side to side, and dance on tiptoes for hours. Each hopes that his colorful makeup and elaborate movements will catch the eyes of the young Fulani women in the audience.

Masks, sculptures, literature, music, dance—all these forms of art express the creativity of the Nigerian people. In Nigeria today art is a blending of ancient forms and modern influences. In this way the arts reflect the spirit of a people who are striving to create a modern, united nation while preserving a rich history of different customs and traditions.

Country Facts

Official Name: Federal Republic of Nigeria

Capital: Abuja

Location: on the southern coast of West Africa, along the Gulf of Guinea. Bordered by Niger to the north, Chad to the northeast, Cameroon to the east, Benin to the west, and the Atlantic Ocean to the south.

Area: 356,669 square miles (933,772 square kilometers); *Greatest distances*: east–west, 700 miles (1,126 kilometers); north–south, 650 miles (1,046 kilometers)

Elevation: *Highest*: Jos Plateau, 6,700 feet (2,042 meters) in the center of the country. *Lowest*: sea level, along Atlantic coast

Climate: varies—dry and hot in the north, wet and steamy in the south. Rainy season is from April to October, dry season from November to March.

Population: 98,100,000 (one-quarter of the population of Africa south of the Sahara). *Distribution*: 26 percent urban, 74 percent rural

Form of Government: military dictatorship

Important Products: *Natural Resources:* petroleum, natural gas, coal, tin, limestone, zinc, and columbite. *Agriculture*: cattle, maize, yams, rice, pineapples, cocoyams, bananas, palm oil, cocoa, peanuts, rubber, timber, sugar, ginger, cassavas, cotton, soya beans, guavas, mangoes, oranges, and tomatoes.

Basic Unit of Money: naira; naira = 100 kobo

Language: English is the nation's official language, but Nigeria has nearly four hundred distinct language groups. Dominant are Hausa and Fulani in the north, Yoruba in the southwest, and Ibo in the southeast. Other major groups are Kanuri near Lake Chad; Ibibio, Ijo, Edo, and Tiv in the south.

Religion: 50 percent Islamic, 40 percent Christian, 10 percent traditional religions

Flag: three equal vertical bands of green, white, and green; the green stripes represent agriculture, the white is for unity and peace.

National Anthem: *Arise, O Compatriots, Nigeria's Call Obey*

Major Holidays: New Year's Day, January 1; Good Friday, Friday before Easter Sunday; Easter; Easter Monday, Monday after Easter; Workers' Day, May 1; National Day, October 1; Christmas, December 25; Boxing Day, December 26; Id-al-Fitr, end of Ramadan—first three days of tenth month of Islamic year; Id-al-Kabir, return from Hajj, a religious journey—tenth through thirteenth days of twelfth month; Od-El-Mouloud, birthday of the prophet Muhammad—twelfth day of third month

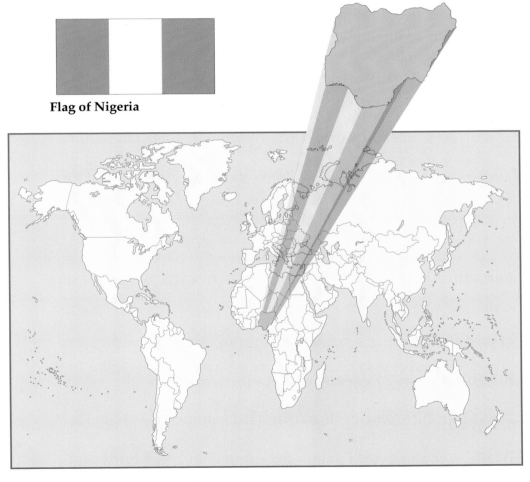

Flag of Nigeria

Nigeria in the World

Glossary

adobe: sun-dried brick commonly used for building houses

ayu (AH-yoo): a popular African board game; sometimes called *mankala* or *warri*

baobab (BOW-bab): a large, slow-growing tropical tree with a thick trunk

compound: a group of houses surrounded by a wall and sharing an inner courtyard

dialect: a form of language that is spoken in a particular area or by a particular group of people

ethnic group: people who have the same customs and language

extended family: all the members of a family—parents, children, aunts and uncles, grandparents—living together in one household

Fulani (foo-LAHN-ee): a large ethnic group in northern Nigeria

griot (GREE-oh): an oral poet, historian, and storyteller

harmattan: a dry, dusty wind that blows from the Sahara Desert across West Africa

Hausa (HOW-suh): a large ethnic group in northern Nigeria

highlife: a style of West African popular music

Ibo (EE-boh): a major ethnic group of southeastern Nigeria

Islam: a major world religion centered in the Middle East, founded by the prophet Muhammad

juju: a style of Nigerian popular music

Koran: the sacred text of the Islamic religion

mangrove: a tropical evergreen tree or shrub that forms thickets along tidal shores

myth: a traditional story that explains the customs or beliefs of a people

nomadic: having no fixed home but instead moving from place to place in search of food and water

oni: the word for "king" among the Yoruba people

Pan-Africanism: a movement to create a bond between Africans and people of African heritage in other countries

Ramadan (RAH-muh-dahn): the ninth month of the Islamic year, spent in fasting from sunrise to sunset

Sahel (sah-HEHL): the semidry region that separates the Sahara Desert from the savanna in Africa

savanna: grasslands with scattered trees

sultan: the king or ruler of certain Muslim countries

tente (ten-TAY): a children's clapping game

terra-cotta: a clay used in making pottery

Yoruba (YAW-ruh-buh): a large ethnic group in southwestern Nigeria

For Further Reading

Aardema, Verna. *What's So Funny, Ketu.* New York: Dial Books for Young Readers, 1989.

Achebe, Chinua. *The Flute.* Enugu, Nigeria: Fourth Dimension Publishing, 1990.

Barker, Carol. *A Family in Nigeria.* Minneapolis: Lerner, 1985.

Bash, Barbara. *Tree of Life: The World of the African Baobab.* Boston: Little, Brown, Sierra Club, 1994.

Bryan, Ashley. *The Ox of the Wonderful Horns and Other African Folktales.* New York: Atheneum, 1993.

Chu, Daniel, and Elliott P. Skinner. *A Glorious Age in Africa: The Story of Three Great African Empires.* Trenton, New Jersey: Africa World Press, 1992.

Enwonwu, Chio. *Tortoise Goes to Town.* Ibadan, Nigeria: Heineman Frontline Series, 1989.

Levy, Patricia. *Nigeria,* Cultures of the World. New York: Marshall Cavendish, 1993.

Morgan, Kemi. *Legends from Yorubaland.* Ibadan, Nigeria: Spectrum, 1990.

Nabwire, Constance, and Bertha Vining Montgomery. *Cooking the African Way.* Minneapolis: Lerner, 1988.

Index

Page numbers for illustrations are in boldface

About the Authors

Hassan and Bonnetta Adeeb are fascinated by Africa and its peoples. Both husband and wife are teachers in Maryland, and in the classroom they share their passion for African history and culture with their students.

Hassan Adeeb received a Fulbright-Hayes Study Abroad Grant to Senegal and Ghana in 1991. He worked with African scholars and deepened his knowledge of West Africa. He is especially interested in learning how Africa's growing cities affect the people who live in them, and he has helped to write a Discovery Television video on the subject.

Bonnetta Adeeb is very involved in developing multicultural programs for schools and communities. She teaches social studies and language arts and serves as a sponsor for Expanding Horizons, a cultural organization for students.

Together the Adeebs wrote *West Africa: A Workbook of Reproducible Readings and Lessons.*